PLAY BETTER GOLF

CURING COMMON FAULTS

Remedy those costly shots

Beverly Lewis

Illustrations by Ken Lewis

TIGER BOOKS INTERNATIONAL
LONDON

3154
This edition published in 1993 by
Tiger Books International PLC, London
© 1991 Colour Library Books Ltd, Godalming, Surrey
Printed and bound in Malaysia
ISBN 1-85501-220-0

Contents

Beverly and Ken Lewis

Beverly Lewis became a professional golfer in 1978 and has twice been Chairman of the Women's Professional Golf Association. A PGA qualified professional since 1982, she has played in many major tournaments and is an experienced teacher. She has been a regular contributor to *Golf World* magazine in the United Kingdom for six years and is the only woman on their teaching panel. She has won two tournaments on the WPGA circuit but now concentrates on her teaching commitments.

Beverly is co-author of *Improve Your Golf* (published in the UK by Collins Willow, revised edition), and has written the other titles in the *Golf Clinic Series*. Her interests include music and playing the organ.

Ken Lewis trained at the Southend College of Art and then worked as a commercial artist. He has illustrated many golf books, working with players such as Peter Alliss, Alex Hay and Sandy Lyle. His projects include illustrating newspaper instructional features and strips by Greg Norman and Nick Faldo, and he works for *Golf* Magazine in the United States. His hobbies include building and flying his own aeroplane.

Introduction

During many years of teaching and playing in Pro-Ams, I have become familiar with the most common fauls that the average club golfer makes. Whereas the other books in this series are designed to help you play correctly, inevitably there will still be certain shots that are your weakness. Hopefully you will be able to identify these in this book, and be able to cure them. Because one swing fault can cause a variety of bad shots, I have indicated throughout where other pages should be read in order to fully understand and cure a problem. Whenever you make changes, be patient, because any change feels awkward at first, and the shots may not be rewarding immediately. Practise whenever you can, and make set-up and perhaps any backswing adjustments indoors, if possible, with the help of a mirror.

And here's an explanatory note: throughout the book I refer to the clockface system, which I will now explain. As you address the ball, imagine that it is in the centre of a clockface. You are standing at 6 o'clock with 3 o'clock on your right and 9 o'clock on your left. As you swing the club head back, for a short distance it moves towards 3 o'clock; then, as the body continues to turn, it leaves that straight line and moves inwards and upwards between 3 and 4 o'clock. Ideally you will swing it down on a similar path so that it approaches the ball from the 3.30 direction, strikes the ball while it moves towards the target at 9 o'clock, and then moves inside again towards 8 o'clock as the body turns through. This swing path is called in-to-in.

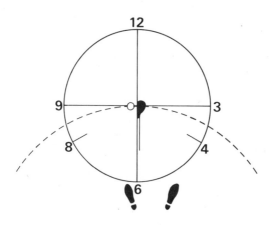

'My playing partners say I stand too close to the ball, but I don't agree with them, how far away should I stand?'

Reason

The problem with golf is that 99 per cent of the time we address the ball and swing in what feels a comfortable manner. We also translate comfort into correctness, as no golfer would purposely try to address the ball or swing incorrectly. For most golfers, standing close to the ball, usually with their arms quite close to the body, gives a sense of safety and security. Sadly it denies them room in which to swing their arms at maximum speed, or on the ultimate in-to-straight-to-in swing path. Standing too close encourages the arms to lift up too steeply in the backswing on an outside path, creating a weak chopping action at the ball, together with the occasional shank.

Remedy

To help you stand the correct distance from the ball, and also to attain good posture, stand upright, and, with your hands at waist height, hold a club out horizontally in front of you. Do not stretch your arms away from your body — keep them relaxed. Now lower the club head to the ground by bending forward from the hip bones. As your shoulders come forward, you should feel your seat going out behind you as a counter-balance. Once you have grounded the club, flex your knees. Your weight should be distributed between the heels and balls of your feet, rather than just on your heels. As a guideline, with medium irons there should be about a fists gap between the butt end of the club and your thighs. This gap increases progressively for the longer clubs, and decreases slightly for shorter irons. You will most likely feel that you are stretching considerably for the ball, but this is to be expected, since you have been standing too close. Carry out this address drill using a mirror to check your final position. Remember that what you feel and what is actually happening, are quite often two entirely different things.

Stand erect with your arms comfortably extended, hands at waist height and the shaft horizontal. Lower the club head to the ground by bending forward from the hip bones, then flex the knees. This will indicate how far away the ball should be, and also give you correct posture. Sighting your left knuckle in relation to an imaginary line across your feet, may help you on the course

Another guideline to use on the course is to sight your left forefinger knuckle down to an imaginary line across your feet. Make a note of where this should be when you have addressed the ball correctly — using the mirror to help you — then refer to this in your set-up on the course.

'To keep things simple, I play all shots with the ball opposite my left heel. Is this correct?

Reason

The ball position should change according to which club you are using. Since iron shots should be hit with a descending strike, it makes sense to position the ball opposite your stance at a point just prior to the lowest point of the arc. A fairway wood shot should be swept from the turf, so the ball should be positioned at the lowest point, or base, of the arc. Since you tee the ball up for a driver, it is best struck whilst the club head is at the base of its arc, or just starting to ascend, so it follows that the ball is positioned at the appropriate point.

Remedy

Irons: stand with your feet together, so that the back of the ball and the inside of the left foot are in line. Move your left foot approximately 3-4 inches to the left, and the right foot the appropriate amount to the right, depending on which club you are using. This process should ensure that the ball remains in the same position in relation to the left foot, i.e. about 3-4 inches inside the left heel for all normal iron shots, allowing the right foot to change the width of the stance.

Fairway woods: adopt the same procedure, but place the left foot about one inch less to the left.

Driver: adopt the same procedure but move the left foot about 2 inches less to the left, so that the back of the ball is just inside the left heel.

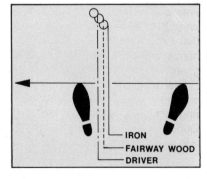

'I grip the club quite tightly because I am scared it will come out of my hands. Does grip pressure affect the swing?'

Reason

Whereas it is very difficult to be exact about grip pressure, gripping too tightly will definitely be detrimental to the swing. Muscles need to be in a reasonably relaxed state to work at maximum efficiency, and a tight grip does not promote relaxed muscles. If there was a scale of 1 to 5, with 1 being light, and 5 being tight, then the best grip pressure would be about 3-3½.

Remedy

Grip the club in your left hand only, then place your right hand on your left forearm. If you tighten your left-hand grip you will feel the muscles in your forearm tense; that is what you have to avoid. Experiment by swinging the club with a progressively lighter grip without hitting a ball. I can assure you that you will not let go of the club. Moreover, you will find that the relaxed hand and forearm muscles will work more efficiently, creating increased club head speed in the impact zone. As you swing the club back, it is most likely that your grip pressure will increase, due to the swinging weight of the clubhead. If you start with too tight a grip, by the time you reach the top of the swing, you will be gripping too hard. If you held an empty glass and then water was poured into it, as the weight of the glass increased, you would naturally adapt your grip pressure to accommodate this extra weight. The same is true of the golf swing: your hands will cope with the pressure throughout, but you must guard against strangling the club.

Feel that your hands are light and firm, rather than tight and firm, with the grip pressure mainly in the last three fingers of the left hand, and the middle two of the right. Once you are confident, your hands, your arms and hands will work in a freer and faster manner.

'I feel my wrists cock too early in the backswing. When should they cock?'

Reason

The problem for most beginners is to appreciate that golf is played by using the entire body. Beginners often feel that it is played solely by using the hands and arms. Sadly this incorrect preconception encourages a weak, narrow and inefficient backswing, which results in erratic and powerless shots. The fact that the hands and arms commence the backswing without the support of movement from the body, leads to an early wrist cock, which sets the club on an incorrect plane and path, and incorrect attack on the ball.

Remedy

Take your address position, facing a mirror. Note that your arms and shoulders form a triangle, which should move away as a unit. If you initiate the backswing moving your left shoulder, arm and club shaft away together, you will feel your upper body turning to the right. As this takes place, the clubhead will remain closer to the ground for a longer part of the arc than has been the case until now. Stop the backswing when your hands are about hip height, and the right arm has begun to fold so that the elbow is pointing downwards. You should find that the wrists have started to cock automatically, but have not yet cocked sufficiently to form a 90-degree angle between the shaft and left arm. The shoulders will have turned through about 45 degrees, and the hips also should have begun to turn to the right.

I believe that the wrists cock gradually throughout the backswing in response to the swinging weight of the clubhead. To the player whose hands have been too active too early, the correct action will create width in the backswing, with a greater emphasis on arm and body action. With shorter clubs you will be more aware of an earlier wrist break, because there is less body action, but the wrists cock must develop after the arms have started the backswing.

10

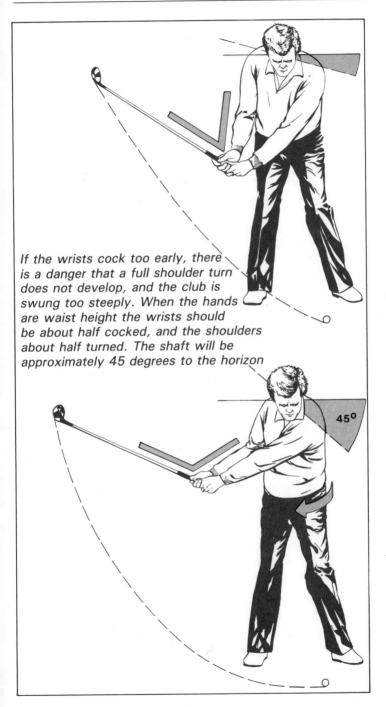

If the wrists cock too early, there
is a danger that a full shoulder turn
does not develop, and the club is
swung too steeply. When the hands
are waist height the wrists should
be about half cocked, and the shoulders
about half turned. The shaft will be
approximately 45 degrees to the horizon

45°

'On the backswing my club head moves on a sharply curving inside path. Is this correct?'

Reason

No, it is not correct. If the clubhead moves immediately inside on the backswing, this will probably encourage the downswing path to be too much from the inside, which can result in pushed or hooked shots. However, it can also encourage the real beginner, who suddenly feels too much on the inside, to incorrectly use the right shoulder area. This action will force the downswing onto an outside path, resulting in a slice or pull. Either resultant swing path from this incorrect backswing movement, does not produce the ideal shot. The move can be traced either to an address fault, combined with the ball being positioned too far back in the stance, a poor initial movement away from the ball, or simply having the wrong concept of the ideal backswing path.

Remedy

Check the ball position, read page 8 and see that your shoulders are aligned parallel to an imaginary line from the ball to the target. Have a colleague place a club across them to check this. Now place a club just outside the ball, parallel to the ball to target line. This will give you a good guide to the correct path. Using the clockface principle, with a 5 iron, swing the clubhead away towards 3 o'clock. If you do this correctly, the clubhead will remain close to the club on the ground for about 6 inches, but this does depend on your height and the length of your club. With longer clubs, it will not remain in a straight line so long, and thus your driver will tend to swing to the inside sooner than your wedge.

However, regardless of which club you use, the clubhead should stay close to the club on the ground for a short distance; it should *not* move immediately towards your right foot. Having set the club on the correct path initially, it then swings inside between 3 and 4 o'clock as your body turns.

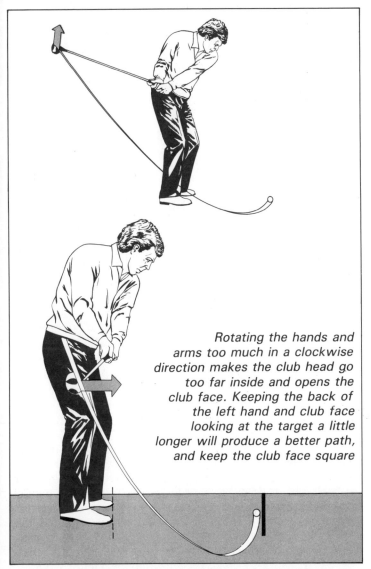

Rotating the hands and arms too much in a clockwise direction makes the club head go too far inside and opens the club face. Keeping the back of the left hand and club face looking at the target a little longer will produce a better path, and keep the club face square

If the fault remains, you are rolling your hands and arms too much in a clockwise direction as you swing the club back. Whilst there is a little clockwise rotation, if this movement is exaggerated the clubhead will move almost immediately towards 4 o'clock as the backswing commences. To correct this ensure that the body is turning as it should be (see pages 10/11), then keep the clubface and the back of the left hand, facing the target a little longer.

'I do not seem to be able to make a good shoulder turn. Why?'

Reason

1 Excessive, exaggerated and early hand and wrist action tends to subdue and discourage a decent shoulder turn.
2 Open shoulders at address, which makes it difficult for even the most supple of golfers to turn fully. The angle of the feet, and lack of hip turn can also create problems.
3 General lack of mobility around the waist will prevent a full or complete turn.

Remedy

1 Refer to pages 10/11, noting the correct address position, and initial backswing movement.
2 Check shoulder alignment, ensuring that when a colleague places a club across your shoulders they are parallel to the ball to target line. To assist the turn, just prior to the backswing, rotate your head slightly to the right, so that you are looking at the ball predominantly with the left eye. Jack Nicklaus has used this action throughout his superb career to help him achieve a good turn, so it must be worth a try. Turn the right foot out about 20 degrees, which will enable the hips, and thereby the shoulders, to turn more readily.
3 Warm-up exercises will be the answer to increased mobility. Place a club behind your neck, across your shoulders, and bend forward from the hips as in the address position. Now turn to the right, then the left. Repeat this action regularly, especially prior to the 1st tee.

Although you see that top professionals have an extremely full shoulder turn, even past 90 degrees, not everyone is able to emulate that. By working on the points outlined above, your turn will undoubtedly improve, but your full turn may still not quite reach 90 degrees. These are the handicaps that golfers have to work around, and if you have trouble turning, be sure to swing back *slowly* enough to give the larger, and slower moving, back muscles *time* to turn.

'My left wrist seems to be very buckled and weak at the top of the backswing. Is this right?'

Reason

The wrist needs to be in a good supportive position at the top, so that the clubhead can remain under control. When the back of the left wrist folds back, i.e. collapses towards the back of the left arm, control is lost. The clubface is turned from a square to an open position, which will require well timed independent hand action on the downswing for the clubface to be square at impact. If the hands are behind the clubface at address, the wrists can buckle at the top.

Remedy

Take normal address position. Without moving your arms, cock your wrists straight up in front of you. Complete backswing and check that the back of your left hand, forearm and clubface are in line, facing between the horizontal and vertical. You will see creases in the skin at the base of the left thumb. The thumb will be in a good supportive position, you will have better club control, and your hands can provide maximum power.

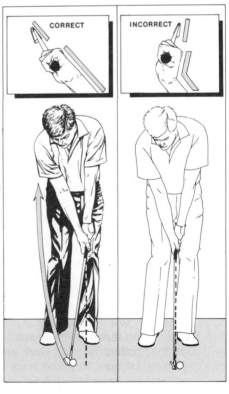

'At the top of the backswing I can see the club head down below my left shoulder. Why does this happen?'

Reason

Length of backswing varies from player to player, but if you see the clubhead at the top of your swing, it has almost certainly gone too far. Unfortunately, women often have this problem, which can sometimes be blamed on releasing the last three fingers of the left hand at the top. If a player collapses the left elbow too much so that it bends almost at right angles during the swing, the clubhead goes too far. The sheer momentum created by too fast a backswing is another culprit, as is too upright an arm swing.

Remedy

Check that the 'V's formed by the thumb and forefinger of each hand are parallel and point between your right ear and shoulder. Keep a firm but not tight grip pressure with the last three fingers of the left hand and middle two of the right, and maintain that pressure, especially at the top of the swing. The swing will now feel restricted, but this is to be expected. During the backswing, turn the shoulders and arms away together, keeping the left arm as straight as possible, but not stiff. At the top it should be slightly bowed, not absolutely straight, as this would create tension. Also check that the right hip turns out of the way; if not, it can restrict shoulder turn, and cause the left elbow to bend. Slow down your backswing so that it feels like three-quarter pace, and consequently three-quarter distance. Try to feel that your arms and shoulders stop moving at the same point in your backswing. You will gain better club control, and quality and consistency of strike. It is also possible to swing the club too far when the arms are swung too upright, so check in a mirror, and if necessary feel that your hands and arms swing more behind your head than above it. When the arms swing too upright the distance that separated the elbows at address increases, so try to keep this constant.

'My husband says that my swing should be shorter like his. Is he right?'

Reason

Because men are innately stronger than women, they can usually make shorter backswings and still hit the ball a long way. However, many would improve their game by making a full backswing with a 90-degree shoulder turn, rather than swinging the club just with their hands and arms and making a three-quarter length swing. Most women lack the power to create enough clubhead speed from a purely hands and arms swing, and sensing this take the club back further than most men. They are easily capable of making a shoulder turn in excess of 90 degrees because they are more supple and have slimmer waists than men, and this bigger shoulder turn will tend to make the clubshaft aim right of parallel at the top of the backswing.

A longer backswing offers them more time to build up club head speed, and therefore hit the ball further. However, if you have a long backswing, it will be detrimental to your game if you lose club head control, or lack accuracy through poor timing.

Remedy

Read page 16 and check that your long backswing is not caused by any of the swing faults mentioned there. You may benefit by experimenting with the three-quarter swing exercise mentioned there, as this will concentrate your thoughts more on the downswing than backswing. The quality of strike and consistency may improve with a slightly shorter swing. If your right foot is angled out at address, square it to the target line, which will restrict your hip and shoulder turn a little, and give you a more coiled feeling in your swing. Alternatively, if your length of swing does not result from any swing faults but is due more to your suppleness, do not worry, but concentrate on swinging rhythmically, and leave the quick short swings to the men.

'My body seems to impede a free arm swing through impact. How can I rectify this?'

Reason

Usually movements on the through swing reflect movements made on the backswing. Consequently the player who in the backswing fails to turn the right side out of the way and who often tilts rather than turns the shoulders, experiences trouble in getting the body out of the way through impact and beyond. This situation is often created by someone who feels that the club should be swung on a straight line back and through the ball for as long as possible.

Remedy

The first point to understand is that the club has to be swung inside the straight line from the ball to target, quite soon after the backswing commences, and soon after impact. In clockface terms, the club must swing initially towards 3 o'clock, then inside between 3 and 4 o'clock as the body starts to turn. The club moves towards 9 o'clock at impact, then inside towards 8 o'clock as the through swing progresses. As the backswing commences, you must allow the right hip and the right side of the body to turn out of the way. This creates a space into which the arms and club can swing. Through the impact zone, the left hip and left side of the body will respond by turning out of the way.

One point to check in your address position is that your seat is pushed out behind you. If the hip bones are pulled forward at address, it is very hard for the hips to turn out of the way, and instead they tend to slide laterally to the right. This sliding action of the hips tends to prevent the clubhead swinging correctly to the inside; instead it swings more on a 2 to 8 o'clock line, producing weak, slicing shots. A good exercise is to place a club behind your neck and across your shoulders, then bend forward from your hips and flex your knees. Now turn to the right, then the left, and you should find that your body moves more correctly than before.

Bad posture prevents correct body action. Good posture allows the right hip to turn out of the way in the backswing, and the left out of the way in the downswing

'I seem to throw the clubhead from the top of the swing. Why does this happen?'

Reason

Throwing or casting the club from the top of the swing, usually occurs because the hands are working out of sequence in the swing. This often happens because the player is too keen to hit the ball hard, and consequently forgets about rhythm and timing and uses brute force instead.

Remedy

During the backswing the arms swing the club back and the hands respond to the swinging weight of the clubhead, until at the top of the swing there is a 90 degree angle between the left arm and the shaft. From this position the hands can be used to add extra power to the swing. However, this power must be contained until the clubhead starts to approach the impact zone.

Therefore, from the top of the swing as the left knee moves towards the target, the *arms* must swing down, so that most of the angle between the shaft and left arm is initially retained. Having done that, you can use your hands to apply their power where it counts, i.e. at impact. For the right-handed player, it is usually the right hand that causes the throwing action, so a good drill is to slide the right hand up the grip until it completely overlaps the left, and is not on the grip at all. Now make a few swings, and you will find that as you change direction from backswing to downswing, because the left arm is in command, the angle at the base of the left thumb will remain virtually the same. The change of direction is one of the most crucial parts of the swing. Keep it *smooth*, and give your arms a chance to play their role before your hands contribute.

Using your normal grip, hit some three-quarter paced shots, concentrating on the rhythm of the swing. Make sure that as your arms swing through impact, your right knee

Practise gripping the club with the right hand on top of the left. This should prevent you from throwing the club, and the angle between your left arm and the shaft should be retained.

moves towards your left, so that at the completion of the swing the weight is mainly on the outside of your left heel, and only your right toes remain in contact with the ground. The player who casts from the top, often has too much weight on the right foot at impact, so do spend some time trying to improve both the rhythm and leg action. Read pages 40/41 which will help you synchronize and improve your leg action.

'However hard I try I cannot make my legs work in the swing'

Reason

To hit the ball your maximum distance, good leg work is essential. So often the beginner believes that golf is played simply by swinging the hands and arms. Leg action is then neglected, and distance and accuracy are lost. Legs help to provide the rhythm in the swing, and enable the weight to transfer correctly in both the back and downswings. Apart from not helping your swing, lack of leg action also puts extra strain on your lower back as you swing.

Remedy

First check your set up to ensure that your weight is spread between the heels and balls of your feet. If you have too much weight on your heels you will not be able to use your legs correctly. Shift your weight towards the inside of each foot, with your knees knocked slightly inwards. As the backswing is made, allow the left knee to point behind the ball, letting the left heel rise if you are not very supple. In the throughswing, make the right knee move towards the left, with the right heel coming off the ground completely.

To improve leg action take your normal address position, using a 6 iron and the ball teed low. At the completion of the backswing lift your foot entirely off the ground, then replace it in the same spot at the start of the downswing. As you swing through impact lift your right foot completely off the ground so that you finish the swing balanced on your left foot only. This drill over-emphasises how your weight transfers back and forth, and how your legs must work to accommodate this action. You may also like to try this without a club or ball; it will help to highlight what your legs are doing. You can then gradually reduce the leg action back to its correct proportion during the swing, holding the finish position balanced on the outside of the left foot, with the right heel completely off the ground.

'I get frozen over the ball, and am taking longer and longer to start my backswing. What should I do?'

Reason

This sort of problem can suddenly creep in to the game of quite experienced players. You may have had a fault in your swing that you have been trying to cure, and end up standing over the ball thinking of too many things, not knowing which thought is most important. Too much competitive golf can also make you a very carefuly golfer, rather than hitting the ball with a devil-may-care attitude.

Remedy

If you have been curing a fault by a number of swing changes, try to work on them in practice so that they can gradually become subconscious movements on the course. Allow yourself only one swing thought, so that your mind is uncluttered. Develop a strict pre-shot routine whilst practising and playing. You should start behind the ball looking towards the target, and pick out an intermediate target about two feet ahead of the ball on the target line. Set your clubface square to an imaginary line between the ball and this spot, and then position yourself accordingly. Keep your hands and arms relaxed, and do not let your grip tighten. As you stand over the ball glance towards your target, but keep the clubhead just off the ground, and waggle it back and forth over the intended backswing path as you focus on the ball. Whether you feel totally prepared or not, hit the ball. Eventually you will feel perfectly comfortable.

It may help you to get the clubhead moving by saying 'One', then 'Two' as you waggle the clubhead, then 'Go' or 'Swing', as a trigger. Do this first on the practice ground rather than the first tee, so that you feel more familiar with the routine. One other good drill is to tee-up several balls in a row, about 6 inches apart, then, without re-gripping or stopping, hit them one after the other.

'I lack the power in my long shots. How can I overcome this problem?'

Reason

There are three distinct areas to look at with this problem:
1 Technique
2 Strength
3 Equipment

Remedy

1 The player who attacks the ball from an inside path, is best able to hit the ball the maximum distance. Providing the clubface is square at impact, you should be able to promote the desirable draw flight characteristic of a well struck ball. So the set up must be checked for squareness, and the clubface delivered into the ball from the 3.30 direction. You are then looking for good clubhead acceleration through the impact zone, which is promoted by lively hand and arm action. If you are gripping too tightly this will prevent the hands working as fast as they can, so read page 9 on grip pressure. Through impact you should feel your wrists straighten so that they are in virtually the same position as they were at address, and also that your right hand begins to turn over the left.

One way to improve your hand action is to swing your hands back to hip height, making sure that your wrists are fully cocked. Now hit the ball as hard as you can. To create clubhead speed you have to use your hands, allowing the right to cross over the left. Do this using a 6 iron with the ball teed low. Also read pages 46/47, which will help with the swing path and clubhead speed.

2 Whereas you do not need to be muscle bound to hit the ball a long way, well developed golfing muscles will inevitably be very valuable in hitting the ball your maximum distance. To improve muscle strength try the following exercises:

To improve hand action make a short backswing where the wrists fully cock by waist height, and the end of the grip points to the ground. Swing to a similar position on the throughswing, using your hands to accelerate the clubhead.

a. Swing a weighted club, try leaving the clubhead cover on your driver (just to start with), then build up. Your professional may be able to add some weight to an old club for this purpose.

b. Squeeze a squash ball in each hand.

c. Holding dumb-bells, rest your forearms on your thighs, then raise and lower the weights. Do this with your hands above and below the weights. This will strengthen your forearm muscles.

d. Practise swinging a short iron through grass about 8-12 inches long.

3 Fortunately today's equipment does enable you to buy yards. Be certain that you have the correct shafts for your strength, i.e. L for ladies, and R for the average man. Try some of the new graphite or boron shafted and headed clubs — although more expensive than steel, they usually add length. Solid golf balls should be tried. The feel with them has improved, and the little you lose in that department, is certainly compensated for by the yards added to long shots.

'As a beginner, I find there are so many things to think of that I stand over the ball and get tense. How can I get over this?'

Reason

Even for the most naturally gifted sportsman or woman, golf is a very difficult and demanding game to learn. It is easy to try to take too much knowledge on board at one time. Your ego demands that you hit the ball well, but during the early learning months, you may often have to be prepared to hit the ball quite indifferently; until your movements start to resemble the smooth ones required in a subconscious manner.

Remedy

If you take lessons or read instructional features, try to incorporate one set of actions before moving on to another part of the swing. I encourage my pupils to break golf down into two sections: the set-up, and the swing. Invariably as a beginner you will be trying to improve some aspect of your set up for each shot. However, once you have done that, forget it, and focus your mind on one or at most two aspects of the swing on which you are currently working. On the practice ground, try to focus your attention on the specific parts of the swing that you are trying to improve. Do not be tempted or misled into thinking that you are there just to hit the ball well. If you improve the component parts of the swing, then the ball strike should improve as well.

You will soon learn whether you are the type of player who can cope with thinking consciously about movements in the swing whilst playing a round, or if you are better leaving most of your conscious thoughts to the practice ground. If you fit into the second category I would still encourage you to concentrate on smoothness and rhythm during your round. If you find yourself getting tense, develop a pre-shot routine and stick to it, so that you invariably take the same length of time over each shot. Incorporate this into your practice sessions as well, so that you quickly become

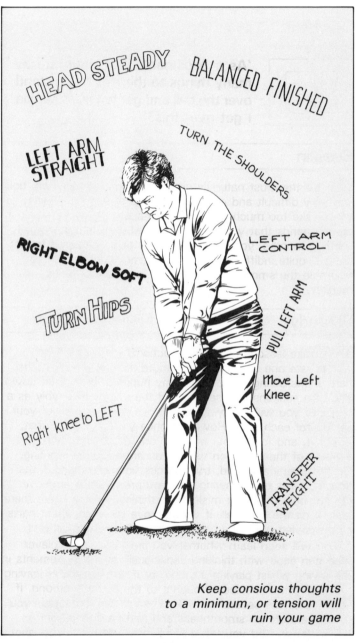

HEAD STEADY   BALANCED FINISHED

LEFT ARM STRAIGHT

TURN THE SHOULDERS

RIGHT ELBOW SOFT

LEFT ARM CONTROL

TURN HIPS

PULL LEFT ARM

Right knee to LEFT

Move Left Knee.

TRANSFER WEIGHT

Keep consious thoughts to a minimum, or tension will ruin your game

familiar with the routine. You will also find that your body will relax if at address you take a deep breath and then breathe out slowly.

Why do I swing too upright, and how can I change it?'

Reason

In all swings there is an inward and an upward element. The former is provided mainly by the body turning, and the latter mainly by the direction of the arm swing. Most upright swings are caused by the shoulders tilting instead of turning, which may be due to bad posture. If you stand too far away from the ball, with your back angled too far forward and your arms stretching, you set the pattern for your shoulders to turn on too steep an angle, and thus create an upright backswing. It could be that you visualize the swing on a straight line, which leads you to tilt rather than turn the shoulders. You might hit some iron shots successfully, but your drives will not be very satisfactory. This is because your swing creates a steep attack on the ball, which suits some iron shots, but not a driver, which requires a shallow approach.

Remedy

Check your set up, particularly the distance from the ball. Re-read pages 6/7 which explain this in some detail. You should stand closer than before, with your spine more upright, and your weight distributed between the heels and balls of your feet. Have a clear picture of where the clubhead will swing, i.e. straight back for a few inches but then it *must* swing inside between 3 and 4 o'clock. Place a club on the ground parallel to the target line, just outside your clubhead, and use this to check your backswing path. Once the clubhead leaves the straight line, the club*face* will start to look to the right of the target. Your shoulders will respond by turning on a flatter plane instead of tilting. A good way to practise this is to hit balls from a sidehill lie with the ball above your feet. This lie requires your spine to be more upright at address, thereby helping the shoulders to turn and the swing to become flatter. If you cannot find a

Stretching for the ball causes bad posture and the shoulders turn on a too upright plane. By hitting balls from above your feet or swinging at a ball on an imaginary high tee, your spine will be more upright, and you will feel how your shoulders turn on a flatter plane, with the clubhead gradually swinging to the inside

suitable lie, imagine the ball is on a high tee and make your swing. Try to keep your elbows the same distance apart throughout the swing. It is quite possible that your right elbow has been flying out behind you, so keep it pointing more towards the ground, and the same distance from the left as at address.

'However much I keep my head still, I still hit poor shots. Why?'

Reason

Most beginners quickly learn one or two golfing adages. 'Keep your head still,' is one of the best known and unfortunately one of the most misunderstood. Many golfers mistakenly believe that if they keep their head still, the rest of the swing will fall into place. What happens, in reality, is that the swing becomes restricted. A decent shoulder turn is unlikely, and the correct amount of weight transference is lacking. The result is known as a reverse pivot, where the weight at the top of the backswing is too much on the left side. As the downswing commences, the weight shifts to the right side, so that very often fat shots occur, and cleanly hit shots lack length.

Remedy

The golf swing is made around a central hub which must remain steady. This hub is not the head, but the large bone at the top of the spine. Using a 5 iron, start your backswing with your head positioned behind the ball, and weight evenly distributed. Prior to swinging the club back, rotate your head to the right so that the left eye is closer to the ground than the right eye. This will assist you to make a complete shoulder turn. During the backswing, allow your weight to shift more onto the right side. This will feel like a swaying motion, which is to be expected if your weight has been moving previously in the opposite direction. From this correct position your weight can now transfer back to the left side, thereby moving towards the target as you strike the ball. Think of swinging around that central hub, and allow a little head movement to develop on the backswing if necessary.

To be clear, I am not saying that you should sway on the backswing so that the hub moves laterally to the right, but when the incorrect action has been ingrained, then this is what it will *feel* like. Ask a friend to hold a club horizontally

By restricting head movement you will encourage a reverse pivot. The swing should pivot around a central hub at the top of the spine so that weight transfers to the right side

just outside your right ear; then when you swing you can gauge if your head moves either way. Swinging with the sun behind you will also enable you to see what is happening. Once the ball has been struck, allow your head to rotate towards the target, so that your throughswing continues to accelerate through the ball, guaranteeing maximum clubhead speed.

'As a right-handed person playing golf right-handed, I feel my left hand and arm contribute little to the swing. Is this correct?'

Reason

A very high percentage of golfers are right handed and indeed play the game that way. All their lives they have performed most tasks of strength and dexterity with the right hand, and so, understandably, it has become stronger and better trained than the left. The question is often asked, 'Is golf a right-handed game?' I believe it is a double-sided game, with both hands and arms playing an important role, whether you are right- or left-handed, and regardless of which side of the ball you stand. What the very right-handed player must do is to train the left arm to cope with, and direct the power of, the right.

Remedy

I believe the right-handed player should put more emphasis on the left side throughout the backswing, which helps to get the body turning correctly, leading to the desired top of the backswing position where the back faces the target. To appreciate how the left arm should work, at address place your right hand over the left — *not* on the grip. Now make the backswing and you will feel the correct action and the role that the left side plays.

At the top of the swing, the change of direction should be made by the left side, which is in a better position than the right to start pulling the club back to the ball. Once this change of direction has taken place, then both hands and arms should contribute power and clubhead speed to the swing. The left arm must continue swinging through the impact zone, with the left elbow gradually bending towards the ground after impact.

By practising the right hand over left drill, and also swinging with the left arm only, gripping down on a 7 iron, you will quickly improve the power and control in this arm. One word of warning, however: so that you do not damage

Practise by putting your hand over the left on the grip, to appreciate and improve the role of the left hand and arm

your arm, start with just a few one-armed swings, and then gradually increase the number.

'I'm told I lift my head when I hit the ball. How can I stop this?'

Reason

I have seldom seen even total beginners lift just their head on long shots. What happens is that they use their body incorrectly and it rises up through the shot in an effort to impart power. Since the head is attached to the body it is inevitable that the head comes up as well. Whilst the head should remain at virtually the same height throughout the swing, on any long shots there has to be a degree of flexibility from side to side, otherwise the swing is too restricted. It is only on the shortest of pitches, chips and all putts that the head can or should be kept absolutely still.

Remedy

The answer lies in learning to swing your arms more freely, allowing your body to move to accommodate the arm swing. This is often difficult at first because the body feels so much stronger than the hands or arms. The most important factor in hitting the ball a long way is clubhead speed (provided that the face and swing path are square to the target at impact), and as the hands and arms can move much faster than the body, they are best employed for the task. Practise hitting shots with your feet together and the ball on a low tee. If you use your body you will over-balance, so you will quickly learn and feel how your hands and arms should perform. When you swing, try not to over-power the ball, but cultivate a smooth balanced swing, letting your body follow rather than lead. Keep your head steady, and certainly watch the ball until it is struck. Then allow it to rotate towards the target. At address your spine is angled forward, and you must learn to retain this angle until well after impact. At the beginning, your swing will feel rather cramped and restricted, but you will undoubtedly start to hit the ball better.

You will also find it helps you to appreciate how the

You must retain the
spinal angle set
at address until well after
impact. Alter that angle
and obviously your head
will rise as well

swing should feel by making shadow swings, i.e. swinging
without the club, just interlocking your hands together. You
will be better able to sense a free swinging arm action if
your body is more passive. Consequently it will not lift up
during impact and neither will your head.

'I have often read that to hit a ball low you move the ball back but keep the hands forward. When I do this the ball still goes too high and way to the right. What am I doing wrong?'

Reason

What you have read is absolutely correct, and indeed you will read that same advice in this book. Where you are going wrong is that when you slope the shaft towards the target, you allow the clubface to open, causing it to be open at impact. Any time this happens the ball will fade or slice to the right depending on the degree of openness. When the ball is back in the stance it is contacted when the club is still approaching from the inside; if the face is square the ball draws back, but if it is open the ball starts right, then curves right.

Remedy

Survey the shot from behind the ball, and pick out an intermediate target about 3 feet ahead on the target line. Align the clubface at right angles to an imaginary line between the ball and this closer target (a). When you take your stance with the ball positioned further back than normal, the shaft slopes noticeably forward so that your hands are still opposite the inside of your left thigh, but the clubface must become *hooded* (b), not open. This de-lofts it, making a 7 iron more like a 5 iron, depending on how far back the ball is played. But the clubface remains *square* to the target line, and consequently it should be square at impact. When you allow the face to open (c), you add loft, so that in effect you negate the act of playing the ball back.

A   B   C

'I top a lot of iron shots or push them. Why?'

Reason

To strike iron shots crisply, it is necessary for the club to be descending still as the ball is struck, taking a divot after impact. However, when someone is pushing and topping a lot of shots, the problems arises from too shallow an attack on the ball, brought about by the clubhead approaching too much from inside the target line. The base or lowest point of the arc of the club then occurs prior to impact, and thus the ball is not struck while the clubhead is still descending.

Remedy

Check the address position, ensuring that when a club is placed across the shoulders, it does not aim at, or right of, the target. It should point parallel left of the target. If your shoulder alignment is significantly right of the target, this causes the exaggerated inside and shallow attack. Be sure to have the ball forward of centre, about 3-4 inches inside the left heel. From the corrected set up, you should be able to produce more crisply struck and straighter shots almost immediately. However, if your shoulder line is satisfactory, you have a swing fault that needs correcting. You need to imagine and then create a different swing path into the ball. In clock face terms, your club approaches too much from the 4-5 o'clock direction, and needs to come more from the 3.30 line. Make sure that the club swings back between 3 and 4 o'clock, and that at the top of the swing your hands and arms *feel* more above your head than behind it.

Check this new position in a mirror. From this more upright backswing, the club will be descending more steeply than before, resulting in the clubhead descending onto the ball just prior to the base of the arc, which will now occur just *after* impact. The club head will be approaching more from the 3.30 than 4 o'clock direction. Read pages 12/13.

'I hit a lot of my iron shots thin, and the better ones lack distance. Why?'

Reason

In the address position the left arm and the shaft form a fairly straight line, which should be likened to the radius of a circle. During the backswing this radius is broken by the wrists cocking. If this angle is not fully restored at impact to resemble almost exactly its address position, then the radius is not completed and the clubhead will not strike the bottom of the ball, but will instead produce a thin shot. Lack of distance even on the better struck shots tends to suggest that the grip may be too tight, thus inhibiting a free-flowing hand action. It is also possible that you have the wrong mental picture of how the ball should be struck, perhaps trying to hit the ball *up* in the air, rather than allowing the clubhead to descend on the ball.

Remedy

Provided that the clubhead is descending onto the back of the ball, the loft of the club will apply backspin, which will get the ball airborne. Any attempt to hit up on the ball causes a thin shot, imparting topspin, which causes the ball to nosedive. Hitting up on the ball also makes the left arm buckle, thus shortening the radius and thereby producing the very situation you want to eradicate. To help improve hand action and speed, first be sure that you are not gripping the club too tightly (read page 9 on grip pressure). Take a 6 or 7 iron and experiment with using a lighter grip to see if you can get better clubhead speed. Practise without a ball and you will be able to hear if the speed improves.

Practise hitting balls but try to stop the club quickly after impact. Although your arms can drop fairly quickly, the swinging weight of the clubhead will activate the hands. Also use the drill on page 25.

A buckled left elbow, or trying to hit the ball up into the air, will cause thin shots. Hitting shots with an abbreviated follow through will activate the hands and improve the strike

'Why do I hit my iron shots fat?'

Reason

When you hit an iron shot fat, you take a small amount of turf *before* the ball is struck. If your drives are hit well you might have a set-up fault with your irons. If your drives are also unsatisfactory, perhaps lacking power or hooking uncontrollably, you may lack left-side control throughout your game.

Remedy

1 Check that you do not have the ball too far forward in your stance. Hit a few shots with the ball more central and you may be pleasantly surprised at the results. The ball should be positioned just prior to the base of the arc. If you play it forward of this point, the clubhead will quite readily strike the ground first. Also check that your hands are ahead of the ball at address, with the left arm and shaft forming a straight line. The shaft should slope towards the target. Re-read page 8 which will give you some good guidelines.
2 Crisp iron shots require good timing. In the swing, your top half, i.e. the hands and arms, are out-racing the lower half, i.e. the legs. From the top of the swing change direction smoothly, pulling down with the left arm and moving the left knee towards the target. There should be a tautness in the left arm and side at the top of the swing, and the correct move from the top will preserve that tautness into the first part of the downswing. You must initially have a feeling of pulling the club head back into the ball with your left arm, rather than throwing it with the right. Try to swing through to a finish, with your body facing the hole, and the right heel released from the ground. To help preserve the tautness, imagine at the top of the swing a length of string tied between your left knee and left wrist. The two must move together to keep the string either from breaking or sagging. Read pages 30/31, because you may

Imagine a piece of rope tied between your left knee and wrist. As you start the downswing try to keep the rope taut; this will improve left side control and your timing

also be lacking correct weight shift due to keeping your head too still.

'I shank a lot of my irons, and the better shots start left. Why?'

Reason

A shanked iron shot is hit from the area called the shank, where the hosel blends into the clubface. Any ball hit from this area shoots quite alarmingly out to the right. It is possible to shank with the clubhead approaching from either inside or outside the target line, but the fact that your better shots start left indicates that your shank is caused by an out-to-in swing path.

Remedy

Read pages 46/47, which detail how to correct the out-to-in swing path, and in addition check at address that there is at least 4-5 inches space between the end of the grip and your thighs with a medium iron. One good practice drill is to put 2 tee pegs in the ground about 2 inches apart, one nearer to you than the other. Address the outer tee, then swing the club and try to hit the inner one. This will train you to keep the club on the inside on the downswing, instead of re-routing it onto an outside track. It is most likely that your right shoulder area has been too active from the top of the backswing, so concentrate on swinging your arms and using your hands, and do not try to swing too aggressively. You should feel that your arms swing more to the right of the target than before.

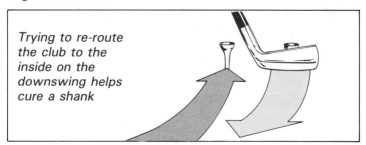

Trying to re-route the club to the inside on the downswing helps cure a shank

'I have great difficulty playing long irons. How can I improve'.

Reason

Because long irons do not have much loft; any sidespin imparted by an open or closed club face is highlighted; the ball curves more violently than when playing a middle or short iron. The lack of loft also makes you try to help the ball into the air. When this happens you fall back onto the right foot and top the ball along the ground. Long irons also have a small head which does not inspire confidence and combined with the longer shafts make the clubs much more difficult to use.

Remedy

If you badly slice or hook the ball, the best advice is to cure that first before you use a 1, 2 or 3 iron. You may be able to play a 4 iron with some success, but your swing needs to improve. The answer could be to make more use of lofted fairway woods as they are more forgiving clubs. If you hit your middle irons reasonably well, then you should be able to manage the 3 and 4 iron, but only the straighter hitting low handicap players should expect to hit 1 and 2 irons well.

Hit about twenty 6 irons shots, then, using the same rhythm and pace, hit a few long irons. Play the ball in the same position in relation to the left heel and just move your right foot more to the right. Either place the ball on a low tee, or give yourself a good lie to help build up your confidence. Keep the swing smooth, and as you change direction at the top of the swing ensure that your weight starts to move back to the left side. You will then be assured of striking down slightly on the ball. Because of the longer shaft, the swing will be a little flatter, so you will not take a large divot. Keep practising, using alternately long and medium irons.

'I always thin shots from tight lies, and am now very scared of them. How should I play them?'

Reason

The main problem with tight lies is contacting the ball in exactly the right spot. When the ball sits on a cushion of grass it seems easy to hit down and through the ball, but when there is only compacted earth, or very little grass beneath the ball, the temptation is to try to hit it up into the air. Professional golfers often prefer a tight lie, as no grass intervenes between the clubface and ball, and so they are better able to spin and control it as they wish.

Remedy

First you need to practise these shots off the course, so go to a spot on the practice ground that is particularly bare and fairly hard. Using a 5 or 6 iron, play the ball further back in your stance, perhaps a ball's width. You may need to experiment to find the best position that allows you to strike the ball readily with a more downward blow. Keep your hands ahead of the clubface, and a touch more weight on your left side; then, from a normal backswing, concentrate on hitting *down*, keeping the back of the left wrist very firm. The swing will feel more punchy than usual, and the ball will fly lower because you de-lofted the club at address. Once you can hit the iron well, try a few shots with a lofted wood, using the same technique. If you need extra height on a shot, play a fade, by aiming your shoulders and feet left of target and opening the clubface. Where this shot differs from a normal fade is that you must still play the ball back in your stance to accommodate the lie. Take enough club for the shot, because the ball will go high and land softly. The left hand must lead through the shot, keeping the blade a little open.

For those formidable pitches over bunkers from tight lies, do not be over-ambitious. The higher handicap player might be better playing away from the pin if it offers an alternative

On tight lies play the ball back in your stance. From the normal position there is a likelihood of thinning the shot Concentrate on hitting down on the ball

shot such as a chip and run. For the better player and when there is no alternative shot, you would find the shot easier with a wedge or 9 iron, but the ball will not fly very high. Play it in the same manner as the fade shot, keeping the head very still and your weight on the left side. The wrists must remain firm and ahead of the clubface through impact and, above all, stay down on the shot.

'My shots nearly always start left of target. Some curve back to the right whereas others stay left. Why does this happen?'

Reason

These flight characteristics indicate that, at impact the clubhead is travelling left of the target, instead of towards it. When the shot continues flying left of target, it indicates that the clubface was square to the direction in which it was travelling. Where the ball starts left and then curves to the right, this indicates that at impact, the clubface was looking to the right of the direction in which it was travelling, i.e. open at impact. You will also find that shots with the straighter faced clubs, i.e. the driver, and 1-5 irons, will curve more than the lofted clubs. This is because the lofted clubs impart more backspin which tends to override unwanted sidespin.

Remedy

First check that your shoulders, hips and feet are aimed parallel left of the target. Also check that the ball is not positioned too far forward in your stance — the back of the ball must be inside the left heel for the driver, and about 3-4 inches inside for iron shots. Ensure that your grip is strong enough, the 'V's between thumb and forefinger on each hand should be parallel and pointing between the right ear and right shoulder. Do not grip too tightly; maintain pressure on the club with the last 3 fingers of the left hand, and the middle 2 of the right. However, do not strangle the club, but hold it with just enough pressure to control it. You must now concentrate on the direction in which you should swing the clubhead; in clock face terms, more from 4-10 o'clock, as a corrective measure.

Lay down a club in that direction and, while standing parallel to the target, try swinging the clubhead parallel to the club on the ground. You should feel that you are swinging to the right of the target. You may well find that most of your shots now fly towards the target, but if some

*Lay down a club in the corrective 4-10 o'clock
direction, then while standing square to
the target, try to swing the clubhead
parallel to this club, allowing the hands to rotate
anti-clockwise through the impact zone*

are still drifting to the right, your hand action needs
improving. Through impact you must have the feeling that
the right hand is starting to turn over to the left.
Concentrate on getting the back of the right hand parallel to
the target line as soon as possible after impact. Two drills
will help: for swing path and hand action see the right foot
behind left drill on pages 48/49; and for hand action see
pages 24/25.

'I always take a divot with my driver. Why does this happen?'

Reason

This indicates that the clubhead is approaching the ball from too steep an angle, usually as a result of an out to swing path. Because the ball is teed up, best results will be gained if the club head approaches from a shallow inside path, with the ball being struck either at the base of the arc, or when the clubhead is just ascending, which will give maximum distance to the shot.

Remedy

First I would suggest that you refer back to pages 46/47 and, in addition, to the address checks there, place a little more weight on the right side, as this will help you strike the ball with an ascending clubhead. Flex the right knee inwards more than usual which will help lower the right shoulder, and put your head well behind the ball. Also be sure that the ball is not too far back in the stance — it should be just inside the left heel, and you should have a strong sense of looking at the back of the ball. This set up will help you to swing the club back and down on an inside path, but do not make the mistake of trying to hit the ball too hard. This often happens when you use the part of your body that feels strongest, i.e. the right-shoulder area, which unfortunately throws the clubhead onto an outside path. Keep the change of direction from back to downswing smooth, and gradually accelerate through the ball.

A simple drill that will help with the swing is to place your right foot almost directly behind your left at address. With the ball on a low tee, and using an iron, you will find it very easy to keep the clubhead on an inside path approaching more from the 4 o'clock than 2 o'clock direction, and therefore from a shallower angle of attack. This will illustrate how the correct swing path should feel.

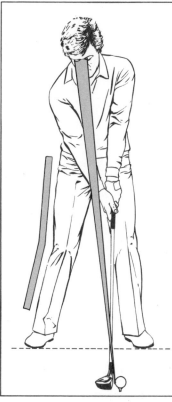

Place more weight on the right leg and flex that knee more than usual. This will drop the right shoulder, and position your head well behind the ball, which will help you to make a shallow inside attack. Look at the back, not at the top of the ball.

Hitting shots with the right foot almost behind the left will help you to ingrain an inside attack

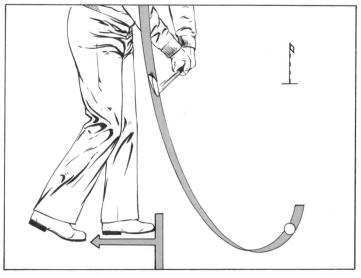

'I hit my driver low and sometimes with a slight fade. Why?'

Reason

This combination of shots is caused by moving too laterally towards the target from the top of the backswing. The sway tends to de-loft the face of the club, and since a driver has only about 10 degrees to start with, it will hit the ball naturally very low. The lateral sway means also that the hands can get significantly ahead of the clubface and leave it slightly open, hence the low fade. The lateral sway can also cause too steep an attack on the ball, and the occasional skied drive may result.

Remedy

Check there is a little more weight on the right side at address. The right knee should be knocked in towards the left, which will help to lower the right side and put your weight in the correct place. You should have the feeling of looking very much at the back, and not at the top of the ball (see pages 48/49). At the top of the backswing, you must feel even more weight on the right side than the left, and the shoulders should be fully turned. Now feel that your arms swing down without your legs moving first. I stress the word 'feel' since anyone who has over-used their legs, needs to feel that they remain passive in the swing.

A great deal has been written about transferring the weight to the left side, but this must be done around a steady central hub in the swing. Feel that you keep the central hub, i.e. that large bone at the top of your spine, very steady as you swing down — do not allow it to move towards the target. You will now get the feeling of hitting the ball away from you towards the target, at the correct height. A good practice drill is to hit balls teed up, preferably with a 3 wood, but keep your left heel off the ground throughout the swing. This prevents you moving laterally, but do not hit the ball too hard as you may hurt your back.

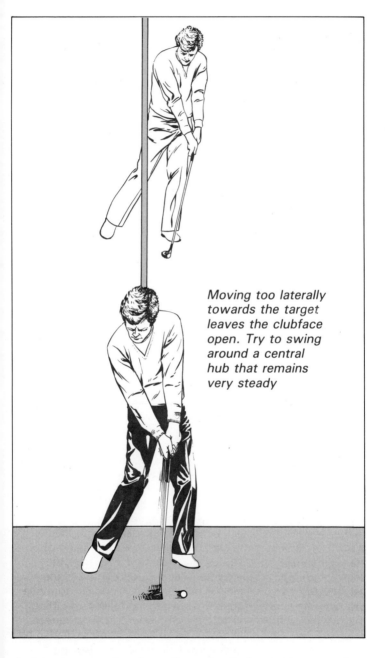

Moving too laterally towards the target leaves the clubface open. Try to swing around a central hub that remains very steady

Just try to appreciate how the swing feels, and how much more behind the ball you are at impact.

'I either thin my chip shots, or hit them fat. How can I stop this happening?'

Reason

As with all golf shots, one of the most important points in chipping is to set up correctly. The majority of poor chippers set up with the ball too far forward, and the hands and weight too far back. This being the case, there are two likely mishits: hitting a fat shot, i.e. contacting the ground before the ball (likely since this is where the base of the arc will occur); or hitting a thin shot, i.e. striking the ball near its equator while the club head is ascending (likely since it is positioned forward of the base of the arc).

Remedy

All chip shots should be struck whilst the clubhead is slightly descending. This imparts gentle backspin, which will initially loft the ball over the fringe before it rolls towards the hole. The ball must be positioned so that it looks well back in the stance, near the right foot. Remember that for chip shots you need a narrow, open stance, so if the ball is placed about 2 balls' widths inside the left heel, it should look near the right foot. The weight must be about 70:30 in favour of the left side, and the hands must be opposite the left thigh so that the shaft slopes towards the target. From this position it is easy to strike the ball while the club is still descending. The swing should be made primarily with the forearms, so that the angles at the back of the wrists do not change. As you address the ball, your hands are ahead of the clubface, and that is how they must remain throughout the stroke. You should feel that you are dragging the clubhead back into the ball, keeping your hands ahead all the time, even after the ball has been struck. To keep the back of the left wrist firm, allow the right knee to ease towards the target. Try to make the back and through-swings the same length, and the whole action as smooth as possible. A good practice drill is to set up and hold the shaft of another

By holding a second club so that it extends under the left arm and to the side of the body, you can develop the correct chipping action with a firm left wrist

30% 70%

club near the head, so that the shaft extends under your arm and to the left side of your body. If you swing through correctly, the shaft will not touch you, but allow the left wrist to buckle, and the shaft will hit you in the side.

53

'I use my 7 iron for chipping. Should I use a variety of clubs?'

Reason

By only using your 7 iron for chipping, you will find some shots that are more difficult, i.e. those where the pin is cut close to your side of the green. Having said that, the 7 iron is a good club for many shots, and by using that club only, you should at least become familiar with how hard to hit the ball for any specific shot. However, to become even more proficient at chipping, I believe that you should use more than one club.

Remedy

When chipping with a 7 iron, the ball will tend to spend one-third of its journey in the air, and two-thirds on the ground. To vary the overall distance, you vary the power of the stroke. Ideally, when chipping you want to land the ball just on the green, then let it roll up to the hole. So if the pin is only 3 or 4 yards on the green, and there are 10-12 yards between you and the edge of the green, the 7 iron is not ideal, since you would have to land the ball on the fringe. This is acceptable if the fringe is smooth and firm, but winter conditions or an uneven surface make it unacceptable. A better club to use in these circumstances is a wedge. A ball hit with this club will spend about two-thirds of its journey in the air, and one-third on the ground. By learning to use even just two clubs, e.g. 7 iron and wedge, you will be able to cope with most situations.

To learn more about how the ball reacts with different clubs, practise chipping using the same strength swing, but hit each successive shot with a different club, working from the 5 iron through to the sand iron. The lower numbered clubs hit the ball lower and it runs further. Whereas the higher numbered clubs hit the ball higher with less roll.

'When the hole is at the top of a two-tier green, I pitch the ball, but without much success. How can I improve this shot?'

Reason

The answer is not really to improve the shot, but to play a different one. Pitching the ball is harder to judge than chipping it. Often the upper tier is shallow, so there is little room for error. Hit the ball too far and it runs off the back; hit it too short and it lands on the up slope and rolls back down. All but the lowest handicap players would be better playing a chip shot.

Remedy

To play the long chip and run the better clubs to use are the 5-7 irons, which should ensure that the ball will roll quite readily. Of course, you still have to judge how hard to hit the ball, and this is made more difficult by the slope. Perhaps one of the best ways to assess the shot is to imagine that the green is flat, but that the pin is, say, 2-3 yards further away, depending on the degree of slope. Set up with the weight favouring the left foot of a narrow open stance, the ball central, and the hands ahead of the ball. Keep the swing smooth and have a couple of practice swings so that you have given yourself a chance to experience how the swing should feel. If playing this shot from, say, 20 yards short of the green, allow the right hand to start to roll over the left through impact which will give extra roll to the ball.

A pitch shot to the top of a two-tier green is harder to judge than a chip and run shot

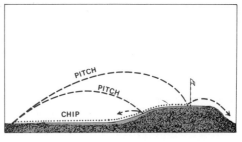

'Why can't I judge successfully the length of my short pitch shots?'

Reason

Once you have to hit shots that are less than a full swing, and this happens mainly with the 9 iron wedge and sand wedge, then you must manufacture a part swing. If you are someone who has very active hands, these part swings can become extremely difficult to judge, because trying to use your hands actively but slowly, requires precision and practice. Without this, the swing becomes either very short and flicky or, from a longer swing, the ball is hit too far. Either way, it becomes difficult to be confident about how far back to swing or how hard to hit the ball.

Remedy

The answer is to play the shot with a more passive-handed swing. Set up with a wedge, hands just ahead of the ball, weight 60:40 in favour of the left side. Now swing your *forearms* back and up, without any conscious wrist or hand action, stopping when your hands are waist high. Look at your hands, and you will see that a certain amount of wrist cock has naturally taken place, but the shaft should be no more than about 45 degrees to the horizon. With this swing you have not created power through an excessive wrist cock. Swing your arms down, keeping your hands ahead of the clubface, and finish with your hands about waist height on the follow through. Your wrists will naturally uncock, and to prevent the right hand rotating over the left, swing your arms to the left of your body after impact. Include a little weight transference and leg action so that the swing develops rhythm.

Hit several shots with this length swing, and you should find that the balls all go a similar distance, provided that you use the same *paced* swing. Once you sense that your arms and not your hands are providing the power, experiment by lengthening and shortening the swing. The pace, and

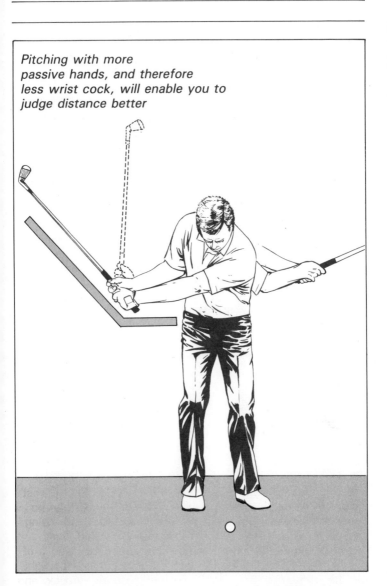

Pitching with more passive hands, and therefore less wrist cock, will enable you to judge distance better

consequently the length of shot, will vary accordingly, but you will be able to develop a consistent shot pattern. For instance, you may learn that when you swing your hands to waist height with a wedge, the ball goes 25 yards, and you can use that as a guideline. Pace out some of your shots, and practise to a variety of targets, so that you become familiar with judging the distance. The swing should feel wooden to start with, but keep your knees moving to provide the rhythm, and leave the hands out of the action.

'Some of my chip shots from light rough around the green seem to fly out and others come out dead. Why?'

Reason

Shots from light rough can be unpredictable. When grass intervenes between the club face and ball, it impairs control of the shot, because it is almost impossible to put backspin on the ball. The amount of grass and the way it lies also have a bearing on the result. When the grass lies in the same direction as the shot, the ball tends to come out quite fast and run a lot. If the grass lies against the direction of play, then this can severely retard the club head speed, obviously making the ball come out in a dead manner.

Remedy

By being able to recognise how the ball will react in different lies, you should be able to play the shot more successfully. Always have a practice swing at a spot where the grass is lying in the same direction as the shot to be played. You will feel the different effects on the club head. When it lies in the same direction as the swing (a), the club will be more likely to slide through the grass, and the ball comes out lower than expected. This, plus the fact that you will not be able to put backspin on the ball, means that you should play the shot delicately, perhaps opening the face of a wedge for extra control. When the grass lies against you (b), it is difficult to swing the club through, so use a little more force. The ball usually pops up in the air from this type of lie, so play it boldly. The best way to become proficient is to practise from each of the lies.

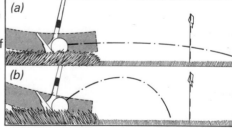

'I hate hitting short shots over bunkers, and always play them badly. How can I cure this?'

Reason

Most golfers fear this shot, mainly because if it is mishit, the outcome can be very penalizing, with the ball landing in the bunker. The mere fact that you dislike the shot usually means that it will be rushed so that you get it over quickly. This may lead to carelessness with your set up and the swing can deteriorate into a short jab at the ball.

Remedy

First practise short pitches without an intervening bunker. Place the ball on a good lie, and choose a target about 20 yards away. Using your wedge or sand wedge, set up with the ball inside the left heel, and your weight just favouring the left side. Choke down on the grip so that you can swing the club a little longer and more rhythmically without gaining distance. Swing your arms up and keep your hands leading the club head into impact. Do not try to hit the ball up into the air — the loft of the club will do that. Feel that you drag the club head back into the ball as you smoothly move your weight onto your left side. Keep your head steady until the ball is well on its way.

Once you can hit these shots successfully, practise hitting over a bunker, or your trolley. Build up your confidence, and when faced with the shot during your round, you will recall how well you have played it. When on the course, do not be tempted to rush this shot. Visualize the ball going over the bunker and then running up to the hole. Have a practice swing, rehearsing the length of the swing, and feeling the rhythm of the shot. Carefully address the ball, then hit it. Imagine yourself back on the practise ground, where you know how easy it was to play the shot. Make your mind work for you, not against you.

'I am afraid of bunker shots as I have no success playing them. The clubhead seems to come to a sudden halt in the sand. Why?'

Reason

Lack of success makes all golfers fearful, and usually the shot is then rushed. When the clubhead stops in the sand, it is often because it is digging in too deeply as a result of the wrong set-up. Moreover, greenside bunker shots are usually not very long, so it is easy to be tempted into taking too short a backswing, forgetting that sand offers great resistance to the clubhead. So there must be enough power in the swing to enable the clubhead to cut through the sand.

Remedy

First check your grip and alignment. The flange on the bottom of the sand iron comes into maximum effect when the club face is turned open, enabling the club to bounce through the sand. So be certain to first turn the face open slightly, then grip the club. Take your stance, with the club face aimed just right of the target, and you body and feet aimed a similar amount left. Wriggle your feet into the sand, working the left in a little deeper than the right, and keeping a little more weight on the left foot to encourage a downward attack on the ball. Position the ball opposite the left heel, and look at a spot about 2 inches behind it. This is where the club head should enter, so hold the club above this point, and not above the ball. From this set up, you can naturally swing across the ball from out-to-in in relation to the target, creating a cutting action on the ball.

Make the backswing primarily by swinging your arms up. Your hands should reach at least shoulder height, with your wrists fully cocked. As you swing down, keep your hands ahead of the club face, and move the right knee towards the left as you swing through. Maintain an open club face after impact by keeping the back of the left hand facing more towards the sky than the ground, and the left arm in control. Your arms should swing very much across your body,

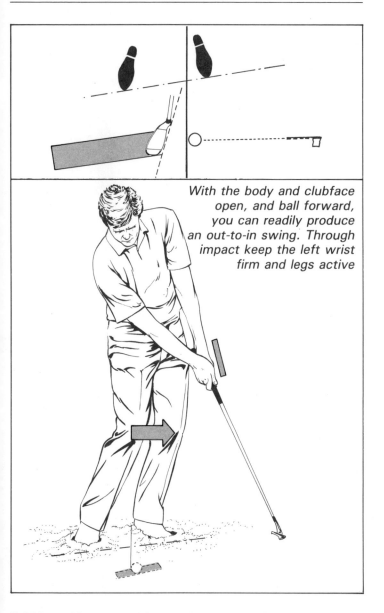

With the body and clubface open, and ball forward, you can readily produce an out-to-in swing. Through impact keep the left wrist firm and legs active

finishing with your weight mainly on your left leg, and your body facing the target. With the correct grip and set up, have the confidence to swing the club through to a full finish, much as you would for other full iron shots. Make the swing full and easy, rather than short and stabby. The exercise on page 62 will help to give you confidence.

'My greenside bunker shots are erratic, I hit some too cleanly, while others fail to get out at all. Why does this happen?'

Reason

As a general rule, the club must enter the sand about 2 inches behind the ball. Erratic shots are an indicator of lack of club head control and thus the club enters the sand at varying points behind the ball, producing a variety of shots.

Remedy

Lack of club head control is often due to too much independent hand action. It is true to say that the wrists break earlier, and more noticeably, on bunker shots, but the arms must continue swinging throughout. Concentrate more on swinging your *arms up* away from the ball, letting your wrists cock naturally. Swing your *arms down*, keeping your hands just ahead of the club face, through impact and beyond.

A good practice drill is to draw parallel lines in the sand, about 6-8 inches apart. With your weight favouring the left foot, stand so that the right-hand line is about two inches inside the left heel. Now try to remove a divot of sand from between the two lines, making the clubhead enter the sand at the right line, and exit at the left. In this exercise you can easily concentrate on the sand and not the ball, and, allied to a greater emphasis on arm action the results should improve. I would also suggest that you read pages 60/61 to be certain that your grip and set up are correct.

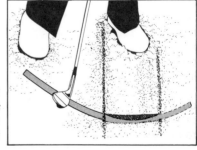

Practise taking a divot of sand about 6-8 inches apart from between two lines

'Why does the ball often hit the lip of the bunker on long fairway bunker shots?'

Reason

Long bunker shots are not difficult, but never be too greedy in trying to gain distance. By taking a club with too little loft, it is easy to catch the lip. Furthermore, since you are trying to hit the ball cleanly, it is easy to catch it a little thin, probably hitting it into the face or lip of the bunker.

Remedy

It is always a good idea to look at the shot from the side, so that you can see exactly how quickly the ball must rise. In fairway bunker shots you should play the ball slightly further back in your stance than for fairway shots, so this will reduce the effective loft of the club. Having taken this fact, and the height of the bunker face into consideration, grip down slightly on your selected club as this will tend to restrict any excessive wrist action and assist clubhead control. I also think a slightly firmer grip than usual, helps to the same end. Get a firm stance, but try not to wriggle your feet too deeply into the sand, as this makes a clean contact more difficult.

One usually advises a pupil to look at the top of the ball rather than the back in order to make clean contact more likely. However, if you are thinning the shot, experiment with looking at the back of the ball to see if the results improve. Although ideally you should be trying to sweep the ball off the top of the sand and just taking a shallow divot, this may result in thinned shots, in which case just think of hitting down a little more until you get the desired contact. Swing in an unhurried manner, and try to finish balanced. Do not be in a rush to see where the ball has gone — just stay down on the shot a little longer than usual. Always err on the side of caution: better to take a 7 iron and get out rather than risk a 6 and hit the lip.

'How should I adjust my bunker shots when the texture and depth of the sand varies?'

Reason

Sand texture varies from course to course and from bunker to bunker, and this makes it difficult to judge shots. When sand is first put into bunkers it can take a time to settle down, and until such time it is very light and fluffy and makes accurate shots more difficult. Depth of sand also varies, but, in this respect, forewarned is forearmed.

Remedy

Your best friend in bunkers, apart from your sand iron, is your feet. Quite legitimately you are allowed to wriggle your feet into the sand to take your stance, and it is at this moment that you can best gauge the texture of the sand.

If your feet sink in very easily, obviously the sand is deep and quite light. In this situation, you should have the club face fairly wide open bringing the flange into play, so that the club head will not dig too deeply into the sand. As it is easy to do this with this type of sand, provided that the ball is sitting fairly well, try to take a longer shallower type of sand divot. To this end you may find it helpful to set up a little further from the ball than normal, weight evenly distributed, and then swing your arms slightly wider than usual.

In bunkers with coarser sand, your feet probably will not dig in so deeply, and neither will the club head. Still open the club face, and with your weight favouring the left side, concentrate on hitting down and through the sand, taking a divot starting about two inches before the ball.

When the sand is wet, firmly packed or shallow, do not open the club face too wide, as the flange will tend to bounce off the sand and you could thin the shot. Try to dig your left foot deeper into the sand than your right, then swing your arms up steeply, and think more about hitting *down* than forward, making the entry point closer to the

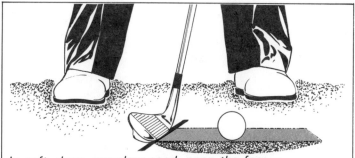

*In soft, deep, powdery sand, open the face
fairly wide, and take a long shallow divot of sand*

*In coarser sand, do not open the blade as
wide, and you will take a shorter deeper, divot*

*In wet, firm sand, square the clubface and
hit nearer the ball*

ball. In extreme circumstances, either use the sand iron with
the club face square to the target, or take the sharper
bladed wedge.

Therefore as a general guideline, the deeper and more
powdery the sand, the deeper the club head will penetrate,
so try to adjust the type of swing you make and the divot
you take.

'I have no confidence with 2-3 foot putts. Why do I miss the hole so regularly from such close range?'

Reason

A high percentage of golf shots require confidence, and none more so than putting. Once technique is reasonable, confidence can bring most encouraging results. However, faulty technique will mean missed putts even from close range, and most cases of poor putting are caused by too much independent hand action. The best putters in the world putt using a firm-wristed action, which allows them to reproduce a repetitive stroke quite readily.

Remedy

I would advise checking the grip first, and if you do not use the reverse overlap grip, I would recommend that you try it. With this grip all the fingers of the right hand are on the grip, while the left forefinger overlaps the fingers of the right hand. Both thumbs should be at the front of the grip, which ensures that both palms are at right angles to the target line. This grip helps to keep the back of the left wrist firmer throughout the stroke. Keep the wrists slightly arched and the grip firm enough to have a steady control of the club. You must bend forward from the hips, so that the arms have room in which to swing, and position the ball just inside the left heel. Carefully line up the face of the club square to the hole, then make a smooth stroke, ensuring that the angles at the back of each wrist and forearm do not change. Try to make the backswing and throughswing the same length, keeping the clubhead and clubface moving towards the hole. Keep the body and head still, until you hear the ball drop or it has finished rolling. A good practice drill for short putts is to lay down clubs on either side of the hole, parallel to each other, forming a track between which your putter will fit. Just practise the 2-foot putts, and you will soon develop a sound technique, which will lead to you becoming a confident and successful putter.

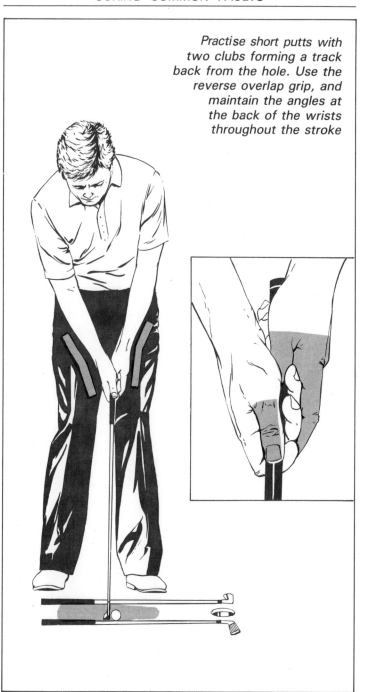

Practise short putts with two clubs forming a track back from the hole. Use the reverse overlap grip, and maintain the angles at the back of the wrists throughout the stroke

'I have great difficulty judging long putts: they finish either well short or well past the hole. How can I improve this?'

Reason

To hit long puts well, you must strike the ball consistently off the sweet spot, and be able to assess the effect of the pace and slope of the green.

Remedy

Take 4 balls and practise on a level green just trying to hit the balls consistently into a cluster about 15-20 feet away. This will indicate if you are striking the balls correctly out of the sweet spot. If not, be sure that the back of your left hand is not stopping at impact; it must remain firm well into the through swing. Length of swing is important too — the correct length should enable you to accelerate the putter smoothly through the ball. Too short a backswing will make you jab at the ball; too long a backswing will cause you to decelerate. So work on what feels a smooth rhythm, which will allow you to increase the length of the putt purely by taking the putter back further. Practise the cluster putting with your eyes shut, and you will heighten your awareness of feel.

On the course, before putting have a look at the putt from the side. This gives you a better idea of the true distance, which can easily become foreshortened. Imagine how fast the ball needs to leave the putter in order to reach the hole. Walk from the hole back to your ball; look at the grass to see if it is longer or shorter than the previous green, and use your feet to sense any slope. Take a couple of practice putts looking at the hole and imagine the pace at which the ball must leave your putter in order to die at the hole.

Trying to sense the strength of any short game shot is vital, and pre-shot visualization must be integrated into your game. Also watch your partners' putts, and imagine how hard you would have hit the ball.

'I have trouble lining up my putts accurately. How can I improve this?'

Reason

Because in golf we do not look directly at our target, whether putting or hitting longer shots, aiming accurately is quite a difficult part of the game. If you asked a snooker or pool player to pot a ball standing to the side, rather than behind the target, he too would have trouble aiming. If your eye-line is not parallel to the target line, this also gives a distorted view.

Remedy

Check that your eyes are parallel to the target line by addressing the ball, then, keeping your head still, hold the putter shaft under the bridge of your nose and across both eyes. This will indicate if you should adjust your eye-line or not. Also make sure that your eyes are almost directly over the target line by dropping a ball from under your left eye. It should fall on or just inside the object ball. You can also check this by suspending your putter from under your left eye. When you have read the line of your putt, pick out a point about two to three feet ahead on the target line, and use that as an intermediate target. All you have to do then is to set the ball rolling over that point, and if you have read the putt correctly, the ball should finish in or near the hole. If the borrow means aiming two inches right of the hole, try to focus on that area, rather than the hole.

One last tip: line up the manufacturer's name in the direction of the putt, then set your putter head at right angles to that name. Remember to aim the name in the initial direction the ball must start, which may not be at the hole.

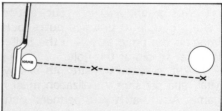

'However straight I take the putter back, I miss too many putts on the left. Why?'

Reason

Although when putting you are standing closer to the ball than for any other shot, you are still standing to the side of, rather than directly over, the ball. Consequently, even though the putter may go back and through on a fairly straight line with short putts, for longer putts it must start to move inside the target line. If you take it back in a continuous straight line, you are in effect taking it outside of the path it should be on.

Remedy

There are three ways to correct this. When practising, lay a club down just outside the putter head, and make a backswing allowing the putter head to leave the line of the club as the backswing progresses. To help to this end, soften your right elbow at address, so that it rests on or very close to your right hip bone. Most golfers putt with a square or open stance. To help you visualize the correct inside track on the course, adjust your stance so that your right foot is withdrawn, giving you a closed stance, but keep the shoulders parallel to the target line. You will now be able to swing the putter back straight but then allow it to move inside as the length of putt increases.

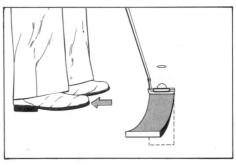

By closing your stance you will be better able to visualize the correct straight back-inside path

44

'As an older person playing golf, I am losing length. What should I do?'

Reason

Once you get older, it becomes more difficult to make as full a turn as a younger more supple player, and you may lose some length. It could also be that the equipment that suited you 10 years ago, may not be helping you now.

Remedy

You can help yourself make a better backswing turn by closing your stance, i.e. withdrawing and angling out your right foot, and also aligning your shoulders just right of parallel to the target. This enables you to make a better turn, and also sets you up to draw the ball, thereby adding distance to the shot. Do not let your stance become too wide as this will restrict whatever turn you can still make (page 14 gives more detail about how to make a good turn). You also need to practise and concentrate on good hand and arm action. Practise with a narrow stance, choking down on the grip of a medium or short iron. Make a very short backswing where your arms hadly move, but your wrists fully cock by waist height, and the end of the grip points to the round. As you accelerate the club through to a similar position on the through swing, use your hands predominantly (see illustration on page 25). This can be done with or without hitting balls, and will keep your hands and arms active and strong.

Do not allow your backswing to become too fast or it will get shorter and shorter. Rely on good rhythm allied to correct hand and arm action to produce well struck shots. Consider using lighter clubs with whippier shafts — ladies' clubs may be most suitable. You will not only be able to swing and control these more easily, but will also create more clubhead speed — because of their lightness and the whippier shafts. Graphite shafts would also be worth considering, because these do help to hit the ball further.

'Whenever I play into the wind I cannot keep the ball low. What am I doing wrong?'

Reason

The most common fault when playing into the wind is to hit the ball too hard. This makes the ball spin faster and therefore go higher. Many golfers fail to take enough club, but instead select the usual club for the shot in hand and try to hit theball harder. Adjustment in swing technique is needed also, so that wrist and hand action become less active.

Remedy

The wind's strength must dictate which club you use, but always take at least one club more than usual. I would rather see a player take two clubs more, and then choke down on the grip. This will give you more control, and will naturally help to restrict the wrist action in the swing. The less lofted club will also quite readily hit the ball much lower. Play the ball more centrally in your stance, which should be a few inches wider than normal, but keep your hands forward, so that the shaft slopes more obviously towards the target. This address position also deducts loft from the club face. (See page 36 for more information on this.)

With this set-up and club choice, you have given yourself a good chance of hitting a low shot, but a swing adjustment is advisable. Make what feels like a three-quarter length backswing, where the wrists do not fully cock, then drive the club through impact, keeping the hands ahead of the clubface. The follow through should be abbreviated, so that the whole swing has a rather wooden feel to it. It is a good practice drill, even in calm weather, to hit some full 6 iron shots and then to hit your 5 and 4 irons the same distance. When driving, tee the ball a touch lower, and play it about a ball's width further back in your stance, which should be a few inches wider than normal. Also stand a little further away, as this will encourage a flatter swing, producing a

To keep the ball low, choke down on a straighter faced club, and play the ball back. With a wider stance than normal and your hands forward, make a shorter backswing with restricted wrist action

lower drawing flight. Choke down the grip a little, and make the same swing adjustments as above, but above all, do not try to hit the ball too hard. A strong wind can knock you off balance, so swing smoothly, and try to finish balanced.

'As I seem capable of beating better players in matches, why do I play poorly in medal rounds?'

Reason

In match play you can have two or three very bad holes, but will only have lost those holes and not the chance of winning the match. You may be a cavalier golfer who goes for broke on every shot. This is fine on a good day but on a bad day in a medal round, a 9 or 10 on a hole will end your chances of playing to your handicap. Remember also that the better players will be giving you shots, and will be expected to beat you.

Remedy

First assess whether or not you take too many chances. I am not suggesting that you play totally defensively, but realistically. Taking your full handicap, assess the true par values of the holes on your course, e.g. a par 4 where you get a shot is really a par 5, then try to play the holes accordingly; you will probably find you make more gross pars. Do not attempt to carry a distant ditch or bunker if it requires a perfect shot.

If you have a bad hole early on, try to dismiss it from your mind. This is harder in medal than match-play, because it is more damaging, but work at it. Most golfers do not warm up or practise before they play, so it is wrong to think that you should play immaculately from the start. However, do have some practice swings before you play, or disaster may strike very early. Use your 3 wood on the first few holes, and then if you are swinging well move to the driver.

Do not try to keep up with a longer hitting player if he/she happens to be your partner; concentrate on your own smooth rhythm. Your putting strategy may need to be changed. In match-play you tend to 'go for the hole' more often than not. This philosophy in medal play can lead to knocking the ball a long way past the hole and then missing the one back.

'When the greens are wet I always leave my chip shots short. How can I learn to judge the pace?'

Reason

When the greens are wet, naturally the ball will not run so freely, so you must adjust accordingly. No one can tell you how hard to hit the ball — this comes only with experience. What you should consider, however, is changing the shot you play from around the green.

Remedy

On all short shots from around the green in wet weather, if possible walk at least halfway between your ball and the hole. Each green is likely to be different in its softness, and you may not be able to see if casual water intervenes between your ball and the hole unless you go onto the green. If there is casual water on your line, you have to play the ball as it lies. It is only when the ball is *on* the green that you may move it. When the grass is wet it is better to choose the air route. At least if you loft the ball two-thirds of the distance to the hole, you should not have too long a putt. So instead of using perhaps a 7 iron to chip and run, use your wedge or sand wedge.

There is no need to play a wristy type of shot, especially as in wet weather if the club contacts the ground even fractionally before the ball, the shot is dampened. You can use a firm wristed chipping action, allowing the club's loft to send the ball into the air. To ensure that you do strike the ball first, play the ball slightly further back in your stance, and open the clubface a fraction so that you still have plenty of loft. If you use a sand iron, make sure that there is a cushion of grass beneath the ball, otherwise the flange will bounce off the ground. Using either club you will have to hit the ball harder than a 7 iron, but you are playing a more predictable shot. Depending on how wet the green may be, play the shot boldly, as the ball will not run very much when it lands.

'What thickness of grip and type of shaft should my clubs have?'

Grips

It is now possible to get quite a wide variety of width of grips. To check if you have the best for your size hands, when you take your left-hand grip, there should be only a small space between the ends of your middle two fingers and the base of your thumb. If the space is considerable, indicating that the grips are too thick, you may experience problems getting sufficient hand action into your swing, and also have insufficient control of the club. If your fingers tend to overlap your thumb, indicating that the grips are too small, you may well get excess hand action and/or lack of control. If you change your grip thickness, remember that using a thinner grip will make the club feel heavier and will encourage hand action, whereas a thicker grip will lighten the feel of the club and possibly reduce hand action.

Shafts and swing weight

The three main shaft flexes in use are: 'L' — Ladies; 'R' - Mens; and 'S' — Stiff. Shaft flexes and swing weights are inter-related - the heavier the clubhead and longer the shaft, the stiffer the flex needs to be.

Ladies' shafts are suitable for most lady golfers, since the fairly flexible shaft helps increase clubhead speed. The swing weight range of clubs with these shafts is from about C0-C8. Some less athletic or older men players often find that ladies' clubs are more help to them than men's, as the lighter weight and shorter shaft are easier to control, and the additional shaft flex provides extra distance.

Men's shafts are suitable for most men players, with the slightly longer but less flexible shaft giving added control and distance. The swing weight range of clubs with these shafts is from about C9-D2. Stronger women may find men's clubs in the lighter end of the range more suitable than ladies' clubs. However, they do need sufficiently large hands to

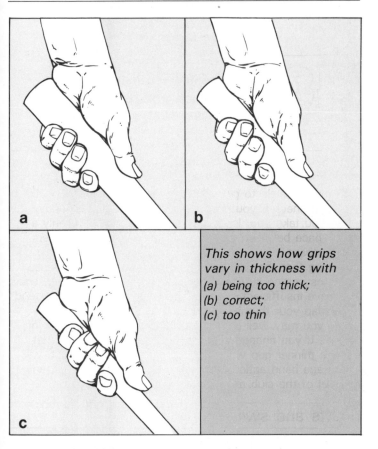

This shows how grips vary in thickness with

(a) being too thick;
(b) correct;
(c) too thin

cope with the thicker grips, and enough strength to get sufficient clubhead speed from the stiffer shaft.

'S' shafts are for the stronger man who hits the ball further than average. The stiffer shaft will increase control of the clubs, which will be about D3 onwards in swing weight.

Beginners should guard against using clubs that are too heavy. Clubhead control is the name of the game, and for beginners, especially ladies who have less strength than the average man, a heavy club makes that control even more difficult.

Swing weight can be reduced by removing weight from the head, shortening the shaft or using a thicker grip. Swing weight can be increased by adding weight to the head, lengthening the club, or using a thinner grip. A good professional or club maker will be able to advise you which club is best for you, and, by a combination of the above adjustments, can tailor your clubs to your liking.

'As a beginner I am confused about which golf ball is the best one to use. Can you advise?'

There is a wide choice of golf balls, and the beginner can be forgiven for being confused as to which is the best. Golf balls really fall into two categories: wound or solid.

The wound ball consists of a small inner core, around which a long thin length of rubber is wound. The ball is then covered in one of two materials, balata, or surlyn. Balata is a soft cover, which permits the club to gain a better purchase on the ball, thus imparting more spin. The top professionals and top amateurs would be more likely to use this ball, because they can control it better. They are able to utilize its qualities to impart the desired spin, and consequently shape shots very readily. Higher handicap players unfortunately more often than not impart unwanted sidespin on the ball, and so their shots would hook or slice more violently. The soft cover also marks and cuts easily, and thus does not last very long. The surlyn covered ball has a slightly harder feel to it, but is resistant to cutting, and will not spin as readily as the balata ball.

The solid ball, sometimes known as a two-piece ball, has a solid core and a surlyn cover, and has an altogether livelier feel than the wound ball. It travels further and, because of its solid nature and surlyn cover, is virtually impossible to cut. It is a more difficult ball to spin, and to control around the greens. For these reasons the better player is less likely to use it, but it is the ideal ball for beginners and most club golfers. The extra length gained by using it, and the fact that it will not curve as much as a balata covered ball, more than outweigh the slight loss of control around the greens. Almost every ball manufacturer now makes a solid ball, and the feel aspect continues to improve with each subsequent model. You may find one particular make that you like more than another, but make sure that you compare like with like, i.e. solid ball with solid ball.

'Why is the lie of my irons so important?'

When you strike the ball, ideally the sole of the club should be parallel to the ground, which enables you to retain the club face in a square position whilst it penetrates the soil. Consequently you are more likely to hit straight shots.

To check the lie of your irons, address the ball, and if the lie is correct the toe end will sit slightly off the ground. This is to offset the fact that through impact your wrists will tend to arch upwards slightly and so the whole of the sole will then be in contact with the ground.

If, when you address the ball, the toe end sits so far up in the air, that only the heel is in contact with the ground, then the lie is too upright. Through impact the heel will catch on the ground and cause the blade to close, sending the ball to the left.

If, on the other hand, the heel sits off the ground at address, then the club is too flat, and the toe is likely to catch on the ground through impact, opening the clubface and sending the ball to the right.

With the correct lie, the toe end is just off the ground

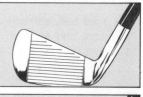

A club too upright has too much of the sole off the ground

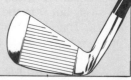

A club too flat has the toe on the ground and the heel off

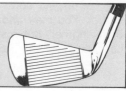

Index